Fearsome Fangs

Fearsome Fangs

Anthony D. Fredericks

Watts LIBRARY™

Franklin Watts
A Division of Scholastic Inc.
New York • Toronto • London • Auckland • Sydney
Mexico City • New Delhi • Hong Kong
Danbury, Connecticut

For Terry Young and Coleen Salley—raconteurs, literature experts extraordinaire, and, best of all, friends!

Note to readers: Definitions for words in **bold** can be found in the Glossary at the back of this book.

Photographs © 2002: Animals Animals: 50 (Howie Garber), 5 right, 46 (Zig Leszczynski), 13, 42 (Joe McDonald), 24 (Raymond A. Mendez), 34, 35 (O.S.F.), 14 (Charles Palek); AP/Wide World Photos: 18 (Chris Pizzello), 19 (Reed Saxon), 21 (Michael Wood); Art Wolfe, Inc.: 38; BBC Natural History Unit: 44 (Mary Ann McDonald), cover (Peter Oxford/BBCWild.com), 10 (David Welling); Brian Kenney: 28, 40, 43; Corbis Images: 5 left, 16, 17 (Bettman), 31 (Reuters NewMedia Inc.); Dembinsky Photo Assoc./Rod Planck: 29, 48; Minden Pictures/Larry Minden: 9; Peter Arnold Inc./Norbert Wu: 2, 32, 36; Photo Researchers, NY: 45 (Anthony Bannister/NHPA), 11 (Peter B. Kaplan), 26, 27 (John Mitchell); Visuals Unlimited: 22 (A.J. Copley), 6 (G and C Merker).

The photograph on the cover shows the head of a timber rattlesnake. The photograph opposite the title page shows a viperfish attacking a lanternfish.

Library of Congress Cataloging-in-Publication Data

Fredericks, Anthony D.
    Fearsome fangs / by Anthony D. Fredericks.
        p. cm. — (Watts Library)
    Includes bibliographical references and index.
    ISBN 0-531-11966-1 (lib. bdg.)   0-531-16597-3 (pbk.)
    1. Fangs—Juvenile literature. [1. Fangs.]

QL858 .F73 2002
591.47 21   200100049988

Contents

Chapter One
Sharp and Serious 7

Chapter Two
Prehistoric Fangs 17

Chapter Three
Eight Legs, Two Fangs 25

Chapter Four
Underwater Fangs 33

Chapter Five
Creepy, Crawly Fangs 39

Chapter Six
Furry Creatures, Fearsome Fangs 47

52 **Glossary**

55 **To Find Out More**

59 **A Note on Sources**

61 **Index**

There is an astonishing variety of fanged animals in the world. Pictured here is a Mexican red-kneed tarantula.

Chapter One

Sharp and Serious

Fangs! What do you think about when you hear that word? Do you picture dangerous snakes slithering through the grass? Do you think about deadly spiders that creep through the night to pounce on unsuspecting victims? Or do you imagine a fearsome monster with an enormous mouth full of **venom**-filled fangs?

Many creatures in the world have fangs. Why do they have fangs? One basic reason is **survival**. In general, the survival of an animal species depends on its ability to successfully reproduce another generation. Scientists think that organisms gradually **evolve** special traits, characteristics, or behaviors that increase their chances of survival in a changing **environment**. Species that do not evolve may die out, or become **extinct**.

In order to capture food or to protect themselves, many animals use their teeth. Some animals have specialized teeth, called fangs, that help them to capture, grasp, and eat their prey. Animals also use their fangs to defend themselves from enemies. This helps ensure their species' survival.

Southwestern Serpent

Look at how it moves silently across the ground, darting its tongue in and out. Now it has stopped and is beginning to curl up. What's that noise? It sounds like a baby's rattle . . . a steady rasping sound echoing through the canyon. Now it's starting to move away. That was close!

This animal, the rattlesnake, is surrounded in mystery, legend, and superstition. Rattlesnakes belong to a group of snakes known as pit vipers. These snakes have small depressions, or pits, on both sides of their faces between the eyes and the nostrils. These pits are used as temperature detectors to locate prey in the dark. From 6 feet (1.8 meters) away, a rattlesnake is able to detect a 0.009° Fahrenheit (0.005° Celsius) rise in the temperature of an approaching animal.

The diet of a rattlesnake consists primarily of small mam-

Dangerous Stuff

The venom from a large rattlesnake can kill a full-grown human in less than 1 hour.

mals such as rodents and rabbits. It also occasionally feeds on animals such as frogs, salamanders, and lizards. Rattlesnakes attack larger animals, such as cattle or humans, only when disturbed or threatened.

Rattlesnakes produce venom—modified saliva that is used primarily for hunting—in a gland behind their eyes. This gland is surrounded by a series of small muscles that contract and force the venom down through small tubelike ducts to the base of the fangs. When a rattlesnake bites, its fangs enter and leave the victim in less than a second. The venom is injected into the prey through both fangs.

A red rattlesnake slithers along in Baja California.

Rattle, Rattle

The rattlesnake's most distinctive feature is its characteristic rattle. The typical rattlesnake has between six and fourteen rattles at the end of its tail. This unique structure is made of dry, interlocking rings of skin. When a rattlesnake is alarmed, it vibrates its tail, and the thickened pieces of skin rub against one another. This creates a rasping or buzzing sound that signals enemies to stay away. Some people believe that the number of rattles can determine a rattlesnake's age, but this is not true.

Because of their sharp and pointy teeth, rattlesnakes cannot chew their prey. Instead, they have a powerful venom much like the digestive juices in your stomach. The poison not only kills the victim, but also aids in digestion of the prey. After a rat or rabbit dies, the snake's venom breaks down, or **digests**,

Its mouth open wide, a timber rattlesnake strikes at a mouse in the Pine Barrens of New Jersey.

the animal's insides. After a few minutes, the victim gets soft and squishy and the rattlesnake swallows it whole.

The fangs of most venomous snakes, including rattlesnakes, are replaced every few weeks. Fangs wear out quickly, and up to six replacements are continually growing in each jaw. A rattlesnake's fangs are folded back into its mouth when not in use.

To Eat and to Defend

Fangs are elongated teeth in an animal's mouth. Snake fangs have grooves or hollow centers through which venom flows. Typically found in **predatory** or hunting animals, fangs are used for two purposes: predation and defense.

Animals with fangs generally fall into one of three categories. The first category includes animals that have enlarged rear teeth. These animals inject venom into their victims as they are being swallowed. The brown tree snake, for example, has fangs in the back of its mouth. After catching and partially swallowing its prey, it uses its fangs to inject its deadly venom. The second category of fanged animals includes those with fangs fixed in the front of their mouths. Their fangs are used to grasp and chew a victim—and often to inject venom during the chewing process. The third class of animals has movable front fangs that fold back into the mouth. Rattlesnakes belong to this category.

Many animals use their fangs to grab prey and hold it. Some animals inject venom into their victim while it is being

Longer Than You!

The western diamondback rattlesnake grows up to 7 feet (2.1 m) in length. The eastern diamondback rattlesnake can reach a length of 8 feet (2.4 m) and a weight of 50 pounds (23 kilograms).

held. Some venom is **hematoxic**, meaning that it destroys tissues and either thickens or thins the victim's blood. Another type of venom is **neurotoxic** venom, which affects the victim's nervous system and often causes death due to heart failure.

Venom drips from the fangs of a prairie rattlesnake.

13

Even domestic dogs have fangs known as canine teeth, which they use to tear meat and to show aggression.

Depending on the species, venom may be neurotoxic, hema-toxic, or both.

Fangs are also used for protection. When a fanged animal is threatened by another creature, it displays its fangs to defend itself. Even a pet dog has fangs, called **canine teeth**, which it uses for both defensive and offensive purposes. These extra-long, extra-sharp teeth can inflict serious injuries. Sometimes just the sight of fangs is enough to scare away any would-be predators.

While you might think of fanged animals as dangerous or threatening, these animals are just following their instinct to survive. Their fangs are important tools that help them to capture food and to safeguard themselves and their young. Without fangs, these animals might die out.

This prehistoric scene is anything but peaceful when saber-tooth tigers appear.

Chapter Two

Prehistoric Fangs

Imagine that you're traveling into the past in a special time machine. You're going back thousands of years to an area of what is now Southern California. Standing on a small hill, you see herds of animals off in the distance. There is a group of small camels drinking at a large watering hole. A few large and shaggy mastodons are lumbering across the plain. Two or three giant ground sloths are eating leaves from the branches of several trees.

Excavators dig up thousands of Ice Age fossils at La Brea Tar Pits in Los Angeles, California.

Suddenly, the roar of a giant cat shatters the quiet of this peaceful scene. The cat leaps from a clump of bushes and pounces on the back of a ground sloth. Its two enormous teeth slice into the back of the sloth. The sloth stumbles and falls to the ground. The cat plunges its fangs deeper into the sloth's throat and rips it open. In just a few seconds, the sloth is dead and the saber-tooth tiger has had another meal.

The scene you just witnessed actually happened. Scientists have been able to locate the bones of these fearsome cats in a place known as La Brea Tar Pits, an area of tar and asphalt in what is now Los Angeles, California. Thousands of **prehistoric** animals, such as sloths and saber-tooth tigers, were trapped in the tar as they came to water and to feed, and their bones have been preserved for thousands of years. Much of what we know about saber-tooth tigers comes from these pits.

The saber-tooth tiger, which lived until about ten thousand years ago, was one of the fiercest hunters that ever existed. Weighing as much as 600 pounds (270 kg), with powerful legs and large claws, it was about the size of an African lion. Saber-tooth tigers ranged across much of what is now North and

California Saber-tooth
Smilodon californicus
The California saber-tooth probably ambushed the larger and slower animals such as ground sloths and young mammoths or mastodons. They were first discovered in the 19th century in a Brazilian cave deposit and are known to have ranged throughout the western hemisphere.

sponsored by:
The Seaver Institute

South America. They lived in flat, grassy areas with rivers and lakes and preyed on prehistoric bears, wolves, camels, mastodons, ground sloths, horses, and bison.

The saber-tooth tiger's most distinctive feature was its two long fangs. The animal got its name from these teeth, which curved down from the upper jaw like the blades of a sword.

A saber-tooth tiger skeleton is displayed at the Page Museum at La Brea Tar Pits. Saber-tooth skeletons can be found in museums worldwide.

These specialized killing weapons were used to puncture and tear at the soft flesh of an animal until it died from a loss of blood. The skull of a saber-tooth tiger was hinged to swing wide open. This allowed the animal a full range of motion to use its fangs as stabbing instruments.

The saber-tooth tiger's powerful teeth might have helped lead to its extinction. The structure of the cat's head and jaws made it difficult for the animal to eat its prey completely. Some scientists think that saber-tooth tigers were only able to drink their victim's blood or to eat their intestines.

Although the saber-tooth tiger no longer exists, its bones and skeletons can be found in several museums throughout the world. Someday, you might want to visit this remarkable creature from the past—but don't get too close!

Reptile with Variable Teeth

The dinosaur is another type of prehistoric animal that had its share of fangs. One of the most interesting (and least known) dinosaurs was heterodontosaurus (HET-er-o-DONT-o-SAW-rus). This creature lived about 200 million years ago, during the **Jurassic Period**. Heterodontosaurus was quite small, reaching a height of about 2 feet (60 centimeters) and a length of 4 feet (120 cm). It weighed about 20 pounds (9 kg) and was comparable in size to a small dog.

What makes heterodontosaurus so fascinating is the size of its teeth. Unlike most reptiles, such as lizards and crocodiles, this dinosaur had variable-sized teeth, each with a specialized

Cutting Machines

Each of the saber-tooth tiger's teeth was lined with a series of tiny bumps that transformed them into extremely sharp cutting instruments—just like serrated steak knives.

Very Long Teeth

The largest dinosaur teeth ever discovered belonged to giganotosaurus (JIH-guh-NAW-toe-SAW-rus). The teeth of this enormous carnivore were more than 6 inches (15 cm) in length.

Pictured here is a fiberglass reconstruction of an 8-ton giganotosaurus found in Argentina. It is displayed at the Fernbank Museum of Natural History in Atlanta, Georgia.

function. The name *heterodontosaurus* actually means "reptile with variable teeth."

Heterodontosaurus had three different kinds of teeth. Like other plant-eating dinosaurs, it had a set of very sharp teeth in the front of its jaws. This allowed the dinosaur to cut off leaves from a wide variety of plants. In the back of its mouth it had a set of broad teeth called **molars**, which it used to grind and

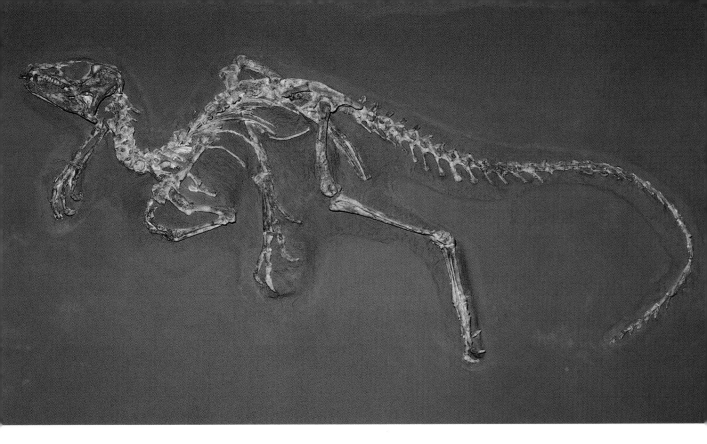

A heterodontosaurus skeleton

pulverize the plants it ate. Along the sides of its mouth was a set of long fangs. Because fangs are not usually found in **herbivorous** animals, scientists were initially puzzled when they discovered these teeth. Although they are not completely certain, scientists think that heterodontosaurus's fangs were used to break the stems of woody plants while it was grazing. This

Bigger Than You Think!

Most people think that meat-eating dinosaurs were larger than plant-eating ones, but that is not the case. Because plants are much more difficult to digest than meat is, the digestive system (stomach and intestines) of plant eaters had to be large. Thus, most plant-eating dinosaurs had bigger bodies than meat eaters did.

allowed it to eat a wider variety of low-growing plants in its desert environment.

Some scientists speculate that only male heterodontosaurus dinosaurs had fangs, which they used when they fought with other males over female mates. In addition, since these dinosaurs typically traveled in groups, several fanged males would have been able to protect the females from meat-eating predators. Additional research still needs to be done before scientists can be sure about how these small dinosaurs used their fangs.

Some spiders have fangs longer than those of a typical snake. The Mexican red-kneed tarantula has a particularly fearsome display.

Chapter Three

Eight Legs, Two Fangs

The tarantula is one of the world's most scary-looking animals. Long, hairy legs, a frightful face, and fangs that are larger than those of some venomous snakes make this animal one of the most feared in the world. The tarantula looks scarier than it really is, however, and is generally not dangerous to humans. There are no known human fatalities from tarantula bites, but severe pain and temporary numbness often occur after a bite.

Really Big

The largest tarantula in the world is the goliath bird-eating spider of South America. This giant of the spider world weighs up to 4 ounces (113 grams) and has an 11-inch (25-cm) leg span. The goliath dines on baby birds (shown here), bats, rats, frogs, insects, small snakes, and lizards. Its 1-inch (2.5-cm) fangs inject a powerful venom that can cause severe pain in humans.

There are approximately 650 species of tarantulas distributed throughout the world, primarily in tropical and subtropical countries. Depending on the species, they can be found in mountainous regions as well as lowland areas. Most of the tarantulas sold in North American pet stores have been imported from other countries, principally Mexico.

Tarantulas live in small burrows that they dig in the

ground. There, they wait for their prey. Tarantulas use their fangs to subdue their prey. When the tarantula locates a suitable victim, it pounces on it and sinks its fangs deep into the victim's body. In order to gain the necessary leverage to sink in its fangs, the tarantula elevates its body up off the ground. The downward thrust of its fangs pins the victim to the ground so that venom can be easily injected. Afterward, the prey is carried to the tarantula's den to be devoured.

The primary food source of tarantulas consists of small **invertebrates** such as flies, crickets, grasshoppers, and beetles. Tarantulas do not have teeth for tearing and chewing their meals. Instead, they regurgitate powerful digestive juices into their victims. These juices pass through the fangs and dissolve

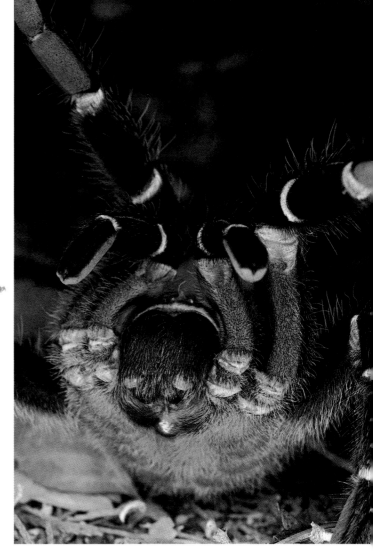

A striped-kneed tarantula rears up in defensive posture. In this position, the spider has the leverage it needs to strike downward with its fangs.

From the Inside Out

The tarantula's greatest enemy is the tarantula hawk, a large wasp. This insect captures a spider by injecting a venom that paralyzes the spider but does not kill it. The wasp drags the spider to its burrow and lays an egg inside the body of the spider. When the baby wasp hatches, it eats the spider alive from the inside out.

A female Colombian brown tarantula feeds on a grasshopper.

Deadly Females

Black widow spiders get their name from the fact that the female sometimes eats the male after mating. Females eat their mates only if they are hungry.

the soft parts of the victim. The tarantula then slurps nutrients from the prey with its sucking stomach. After its meal is done, the tarantula leaves behind the undigested carcass of the victim.

Small but Deadly

The black widow spider is considered the most venomous spider in North America. There are about six species of black widow spiders found throughout the world. Two species are native to the United States, and they can be found in every state except Alaska and Hawaii. This spider's most remarkable physical feature is the red hourglass shape on its belly. Black widows build their webs in abandoned buildings, hollow logs, and other cool places. There they wait for flies or other insects to fly into their webs.

Using its sharp, powerful fangs, the black widow stabs a trapped victim. The fangs' design allows the spider to pierce, hold, and tear a victim. When the victim is subdued, the spider injects venom through its fangs and into the body of the prey. This liquid softens the internal organs of the victim. After an hour or so, the insides are soupy enough for the spider to suck them out.

Black widow spiders are dangerous not only to certain types of insects, but also to each other. When spiderlings first hatch, they have very little to eat except one another. Until they are old enough to build their own webs, larger spiderlings often eat their smaller brothers and sisters. Typically, less than 25 percent of newborn black widow spiders survive to adulthood.

The black widow spider has an easily recognizable hourglass shape on its belly.

Different Types, Different Sizes

There are about thirty thousand species of spiders worldwide. The smallest spider has a leg span of 0.5 millimeter—about the size of the period at the end of this sentence. The largest has a leg span of 10 inches (25 cm)—about the size of a dinner plate. Fewer than thirty species have venom that is poisonous to humans.

Although black widow spiders usually avoid humans, they are very harmful when they do come into contact with people. The bite of a female black widow can be fatal, particularly to the young and the elderly. About one in twenty people bitten by a black widow dies. Survivors frequently suffer from nausea, vomiting, abdominal pain, fever, and temporary paralysis. The venom of a black widow spider is fifteen times more deadly than a rattlesnake's poison.

Down Under

One of the most dangerous spiders in the world is the Sydney funnel web spider. This creature is found in a very limited area: a radius of 100 miles (160 kilometers) from Sydney, Australia. It is relatively large—about 2 inches (5 cm) long—and is greatly feared by people in Australia.

The funnel web spider has two massive fangs at the front of its head. When attacking prey or defending itself, it rears up on its hind legs, raises its head, and exposes its fangs. It stabs its prey by moving its head in a downward motion, and then it injects venom into the victim. The spider makes this motion several times. This repeated downward motion is unusual for spiders. The fangs of most spiders are turned to face each other, and they move from side to side in a pinching motion. The terrible teeth of a funnel web spider are strong and sharp enough to penetrate a human fingernail.

The funnel web spider has a pair of venom-filled glands at the base of its fangs. When the spider bites, venom flows from

Wicked Weapons

Most spiders' fangs are the end parts of their paired jaws, known as **chelicerae**. When muscles in the spider's venom glands contract, venom is injected through the chelicerae.

its glands into a tiny duct in the center of each fang. At the tip of each fang is a tiny hole through which the venom exits. The attack takes less than a second, and the venom begins its work immediately.

Without proper medical treatment, the bite of a funnel web spider is fatal to humans. Symptoms include muscular twitching, a rapid increase in heart rate, and dangerously high blood pressure. The victim may also vomit and lose consciousness. After about 2 hours, severe cardiac failure occurs.

Deadly Males

The venom of a male funnel web spider is five times more toxic than that of a female.

At the Australian Reptile Park in Gosford, Australia, a funnel web spider rears up as a scientist attempts to milk its venom.

A viperfish closes in on its hatchetfish prey in the depths of the ocean.

Chapter Four

Underwater Fangs

The viperfish is not an animal that you are likely to catch when you go fishing or visit an aquarium. For one thing, the viperfish is a very shy creature. For another, it lives so far beneath the surface of the ocean that it is rarely seen by anyone.

The viperfish looks like an enormous sea monster lurking in the ocean and waiting to prey upon ships or large sea creatures. In fact, this fascinating animal is relatively small—about 6 to 12 inches

Via organs along their bodies, viperfish create their own light in a pitch-black world.

(15 to 30 cm) long. It has a slender build, with a rather small head and a very strong lower jaw.

It is the viperfish's lower jaw that puts it in the category of fearsome fangs. Its fangs project on either side of its jaw and are barbed at the tips, a feature that helps the viperfish hold fast to any prey it captures. When it locates another fish, the viperfish lunges at its prey and seizes it in its wide, fang-filled mouth. The viperfish's teeth hold fast to the victim while it

34

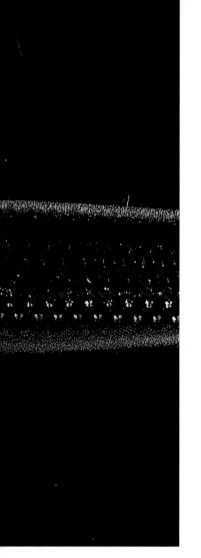

begins the swallowing process. The lower jaw juts forward and makes the viperfish look like its head is separating from its body. This unusual action makes the fish appear to be almost double its normal size. It also allows the viperfish to swallow animals much bigger than itself.

Although it lives in darkness, the viperfish has unique access to light. Along the sides of its body are double rows of light organs. These lights are supplemented with another 350 tiny light organs in the roof of the viperfish's mouth and on the lower surface of its eyeballs. The blinking of these lights attracts the **crustaceans** and small fish that make up the viperfish's diet.

In the Deep Dark Sea

It looks like a swimming nightmare—a creature so terrible and vicious that it could tear apart anything or anyone in its way. It is not something you would want to meet on a dark and scary night. What is this creature? It is a fangtooth.

The fangtooth is an unbelievably strange-looking fish that appears to be more terrible than it actually is. Found around

the world, it is one of a group of fish that lives primarily in the depths of the ocean. The fangtooth lives 1 mile (1.6 km) or more below the ocean's surface in a place of enormous water pressure, no sunlight, and very little vegetation. Few organisms—plant, animal, or otherwise—can live at these depths.

The most distinguishing feature of this deep-sea dweller is its fangs, which are elongated and menacing. The fangtooth's mouth is filled with an array of different-sized fangs. The fangtooth is not as dangerous as it appears, however. This fish subsists entirely on a diet of small crustaceans and tiny fish.

Scientists still do not know the purpose of its fearsome fangs.

The body of an adult fangtooth is short and deep. Its head makes up a large proportion of its body. A young fangtooth has a series of long spines covering its head, while an adult fish does not. Until recently, it was thought that the adults and the young fish were members of two separate species, simply because they looked so remarkably different. Recent explorations into the depths of the ocean, where more of these fish are being collected, have revealed the similarities between young and old specimens.

Small Body, Big Bite

The fangtooth is a relatively small fish. The longest fangtooth on record is only 6.5 inches (16.5 cm) in length.

A black mamba winds around a branch in Botswana, Africa.

Chapter Five

Creepy, Crawly Fangs

How fast can you run? About 5 miles (8 km) per hour, perhaps? You might be a good runner now, but how fast do you think you would run if you were being pursued by one of the world's fastest *and* most poisonous animals—the black mamba? This African snake is one of the most feared animals in the world.

The black mamba inhabits most parts of central and southern Africa. Many scientists consider the black mamba to be the fastest snake in the entire world. It

Quick Killer

Two drops of the poison in a black mamba's venomous bite can kill a full-grown human in less than 10 minutes.

normally travels at a speed of 7 miles (11 km) per hour, but it has been clocked in short bursts of speed at 15 miles (24 km) per hour—a speed much faster than most people can run. Growing to lengths of 14 feet (4.3 m), the black mamba is the second-largest poisonous snake in the world.

Although black mambas typically avoid humans, they are known to be aggressive, particularly when their territory is being invaded. They attack when hungry and when threat-

When threatened, the black mamba rears up in an imposing threat display.

ened. When a black mamba strikes, it rears up its head to a height of 4 to 6 feet (1.2 to 1.8 m) and lashes out with lightning speed. It often sinks its two fangs into its victim so quickly that the prey never sees the strike.

The snake's venom acts quickly on the victim's breathing and heartbeat. Breathing becomes very difficult, and the heart rate becomes wild and erratic. The victim becomes dizzy and usually dies of respiratory failure. Although an **antivenin** is available to counteract the effects of the mamba's poison, a person's survival often depends on how rapidly he can be taken to a hospital. Since most human encounters with mambas are deep in the African wilderness, the death rate of humans attacked by mambas is close to 100 percent.

Desert Dwellers

Gila monsters are found primarily in the desert regions of the southwestern United States and northern Mexico. This animal is best known for its bite. Like most predators, gila monsters rarely attack humans—and when they do, it is only in defense of their territory. Despite what many people believe, gila monsters are not aggressive to humans. In fact, they would rather run away from people than attack them.

An adult gila monster is about 15 inches (40 cm) in length and has brown, black, and orange skin. Although it is usually slow-moving, it is capable of lightning-fast movements when provoked. Primarily **nocturnal**, or active at night, it lives in rocky areas, where it hides among rock ledges.

Even lizards can have fangs. Pictured here is a gila monster in Arizona.

The gila monster subdues small mammals and birds with its venom, which is located in salivary glands in the rear of its lower jaw. When a gila monster catches a victim, its venom empties into a groove along the inner edge of its lips and flows into grooves in its upper and lower fangs. The gila then uses its fangs to chew the poison into the victim's flesh.

Stand Back!

Cobras are found throughout the Philippines and in Africa, Australia, and Asia. Their reputation as an extremely deadly creature is well deserved. They are best known for their intimidating behavior and fatal bites.

Cobras are classified as venomous snakes. Cobra venom is a neurotoxin that acts on the nervous system to cause paralysis, nausea, breathing difficulties, and sometimes death. Cobra bites are fatal to humans only about 10 percent of the time. Deaths are due primarily to heart and breathing failure.

A cobra's venom is secreted from glands that lie just below its eyes. The venom runs down ducts to two fangs that grow from the front of the upper jaw. These fangs are similar to the needles that a doctor uses to give shots. A cobra's fangs are designed to puncture a victim's flesh and to inject a deadly poison as rapidly as possible.

In Africa, two types of cobras—ringhals and black-necked cobras—are known as spitting cobras because they spit at

An Indian cobra's inflated hood warns of a deadly weapon—its fangs.

World's Largest Snake

The king cobra is the world's largest venomous snake. Most are about 13 feet (4 m) long, but one was once measured at 18 feet (5.6 m) in length. Pictured here is a young king cobra.

enemies when they are threatened. Most cobra fangs have a canal through which venom passes. Just before the tip of a spitting cobra's fang, however, the canal turns up sharply and ends at the front of the fang. When surprised, this cobra rears up, opens its mouth, and forces venom out of its fangs and onto its victim. Strong muscles surrounding the snake's poison gland push out the poison.

A spitting cobra aims its spray at the eyes of its victim. A powerful spitter, it is remarkably accurate at distances of more

A Mozambique spitting cobra forces venom up and out through its fangs.

than 7 feet (2 m). The venom causes intense pain and can even blind the attacker. It is crucial to wash off a spitting cobra's venom soon after an attack.

The short-tailed shrew is one of two venomous mammals in the world.

Chapter Six

Furry Creatures, Fearsome Fangs

The short-tailed shrew is a mouselike animal about 5 inches (13 cm) long. It is a member of a family of animals known as **insectivores**, which feed primarily on insects and other small invertebrates (animals without backbones). Short-tailed

A Brief Life

Shrews have the shortest life span of any group of mammals. Typically, they only live twelve to eighteen months.

To keep up with its fast metabolism, a short-tailed shrew must eat twice its body weight in food every day.

shrews, like other shrews, are highly active animals with an especially fast **metabolism**, which is the rate at which a body breaks down and uses food. As a result, they need to spend a great deal of their waking hours eating. Shrews are so active that they must eat nearly twice their own body weight in food every 24 hours.

The short-tailed shrew is known to deviate from its regular diet of insects to attack, kill, and eat mice. When shrews attack mice, they kill their victims by biting either the neck or the head. Special glands located in the back of the jaw produce a venom that is carried by ducts to the base of two large fangs, each of which has a deep groove. The poison flows along these grooves and is injected into the victim's wound. The venom acts rapidly on the nervous system of the prey, which soon becomes paralyzed.

A shrew's fangs allow it to capture and kill a wide assortment of small animals. Although the venom it injects through its fangs is relatively harmless to humans, that is not the case with mice. In fact, there is enough venom in the glands of a short-tailed shrew to kill nearly two hundred mice at the same time. That's a lot of meals!

Shrews are one of two venomous mammals in the world. The other mammal, the duckbill platypus, does not have fangs. Instead, it has venomous spurs on its feet. The platypus's spurs are used for defensive purposes.

Upper to Lower

The fangs of most animals, such as snakes, are located in the upper jaw. Those of short-tailed shrews, however, are located in the lower jaw.

Big, Bad, and Grizzly

Grizzly bears are one of eight different species of bears found throughout the world. They are named after the light-colored hairs on their backs and shoulders. When seen from a distance, these hairs give the bear a grizzled, gray-looking appearance.

Grizzly bears are **omnivorous**, meaning that they eat both plants and meat. They use their large, flat molars to grind up plants and their long, sharp canine teeth to kill prey and to tear apart flesh. It is their canine teeth that make them so dangerous to other animals. Grizzlies generally feed on fawns and the calves of moose, elk, and caribou.

When a grizzly bear is about to attack, it lowers its head, flattens its ears, and makes a series of threatening snorts or growls. It then pounces upon its victim and kills it with its teeth. The bite of the grizzly is capable of crushing heavy bones

The fanged snarl of a grizzly bear is enough to ward off most would-be attackers.

and severing vital arteries. Grizzlies are powerful enough to kill humans, although attacks on humans are infrequent.

Scientists determine the age of a grizzly bear by taking a cross section of one of its canine teeth. Grizzly teeth have rings, just like the rings on a tree. A new layer of enamel is added for each year of a grizzly's life.

Today, grizzly bears can be found throughout Alaska, western Canada, Idaho, and northwestern Montana. Up until 150 years ago, their range extended across the western half of North America and as far south as northern Mexico. Now the grizzly population is reduced to just a few thousand individuals.

A Most Mysterious Creature

One of the most notorious of all animals is the vampire bat, which lives in the tropical and subtropical regions of the Americas. A tiny animal, it grows to a length of 2 to 3 inches (5 to 8 cm) and weighs only about 1 to 2 ounces (25 to 55 g). During the day, vampire bats hang upside down in the back of large caves or old mines. At night, they leave their roosts and search out prey. Most often they attack large animals such as horses, cows, mules, and goats, although they also attack small wild animals and even chickens. They have even been known to attack humans.

The vampire bat sneaks up when its victim is asleep and makes a quick bite on the victim's neck or leg with its razor-edged fangs. The incision is done so precisely that the victim never feels it. Using its grooved muscular tongue, the vampire bat laps up the blood that flows from the wound. Blood is its entire diet—it eats absolutely no solid food!

While the bite of a vampire bat is seldom life-threatening, these animals are carriers of one of the most dangerous diseases of all—rabies. Rabies kills millions of animals worldwide every year. This is the major reason why people of the tropics fear this fanged creature.

Glossary

antivenin—a medicine used to counteract the effects of venom

canine teeth—sharp, pointed teeth used for puncturing and cutting

chelicerae—the front parts of a spider's jaw. In some spider species, the chelicerae are specialized as fangs.

crustaceans—animals with a hard shell, such as lobsters and shrimp

digest—to break down food so that it can be swallowed and absorbed

environment—the natural surroundings of an area, including air, land, water, and organisms

evolve—to change over time

extinct—no longer existing

fangs—elongated teeth, typically located in the front of the mouth

hematoxic—poisonous to tissues or to blood

herbivorous—eating only plants

insectivores—animals that feed primarily on insects

invertebrates—animals without backbones

Jurassic Period—the period of Earth's history that lasted between 208 and 146 millions years ago

metabolism—the rate at which a body breaks down and uses food

molars—flat teeth used for grinding food

neurotoxic—poisonous to the nerves or to nervous tissue

nocturnal—active at night

omnivorous—eating both plants and animals

predatory—tending to hunt and eat other animals

prehistoric—occurring before recorded time (or before humans appeared on Earth)

survival—the ability of a species to reproduce another generation

venom—a poison produced inside the body of an animal

To Find
Out More

Books

Dixon, Dougal. *Dougal Dixon's Dinosaurs*. Honesdale, PA: Boyds Mills Press, 1998.

Else, George. *Insects and Spiders*. New York: Time-Life Books, 1997.

Fredericks, Anthony D. *Cannibal Animals: Animals That Eat Their Own Kind*. New York: Franklin Watts, 1999.

———— and Sneed Collard. *Amazing Animals*. Minnetonka, MN: NorthWord Press, 2000.

Little, Jocelyn. *World's Strangest Animal Facts*. New York: Sterling Publishing, 1994.

Pringle, Laurence. *Animal Monsters: The Truth About Scary Creatures.* New York: Marshall Cavendish, 1997.

Seidensticker, John, and Susan Lumpkin. *Dangerous Animals.* New York: Time-Life Books, 1995.

Tomb, Howard. *Living Monsters: The World's Most Dangerous Animals.* New York: Simon and Schuster, 1990.

Videos

King Cobra, National Geographic Society.

United Snakes of America, National Geographic Society.

Webs of Intrigue, National Geographic Society.

CD-ROMs

Discovering Endangered Wildlife (Lyriq International Corp., Cheshire, CT). IBM.

Food Chains and Webs (Cyber Ed Inc., Paradise, CA). IBM & Macintosh.

Microsoft Dangerous Creatures (Microsoft Corp., Redmond, WA). IBM & Macintosh.

The San Diego Zoo Presents the Animals 2.0 (Mindscape, Novato, CA). IBM & Macintosh.

Organizations and Online Sites

Defenders of Wildlife
1101 Fourteenth Street NW, Suite 1400
Washington, D.C. 20005
http://www.defenders.org
Defenders of Wildlife is an organization dedicated to the protection of all wild animals and plants in their natural environment.

National Audubon Society
700 Broadway
New York, NY 10003
http://www.audubon.org
The National Audubon Society focuses on research and education that helps protect and save threatened ecosystems throughout the country.

National Wildlife Federation
1400 Sixteenth Street NW
Washington, D.C. 20036
http://www.nwf.org/
The National Wildlife Federation works to promote environmental awareness and to help people conserve natural resources.

Wildlife Conservation Society
2300 Southern Blvd.
Bronx, NY 10460
http://wcs.org/news
This group is dedicated to preserving biodiversity, teaching ecology, and inspiring care for all wildlife.

Young Entomologists' Society, Inc.
6907 West Grand River Avenue
Lansing, MI 48906-9131
http://members.aol.com/YESsales/BOW.html
This organization provides young scientists with publications, programs, and information about all types of insects.

A Note on Sources

I first became interested in fanged animals when I was teaching a unit on bats many years ago. I realized that many people, including my students, had some misperceptions about these creatures. Later, as I was working on another children's book—*Cannibal Animals: Animals That Eat Their Own Kind*—I learned more about animals with fangs. I was fascinated by the different species of animals, from fish to mammals, that have fangs. I thought that readers, such as you, might also be interested in these amazing creatures.

I wanted to learn more, so I began reading lots of articles and lots of books. Some of my favorite science magazines include *National Wildlife*, *International Wildlife*, *Audubon*, *Discover*, and *Nature Conservancy*. Books I read include *Spineless Wonders* and *Every Creeping Thing* by Richard Conniff, *Waiting for Aphrodite* by Sue Hubbell, *The Flight of the Iguana* and

Natural Acts by David Quammen, and *The Way Nature Works*, edited by Clifford Bishop.

To locate more specific information about individual animal species, I searched on the Internet. I relied on Web sites created and maintained by colleges, universities, or other well-known organizations. I usually avoid information from personal Web sites because it may not be reliable.

Next, I talked to reference and college librarians in several different libraries. They helped me find many kinds of resource materials. Since I teach full-time at York College in York, Pennsylvania, I asked my colleagues in the biology department lots of questions. I also visited zoos, wildlife preserves, and aquariums to observe animals and to ask more questions. This extensive research was necessary to make sure that the information in this book is accurate, thorough, and up-to-date.

—*Anthony D. Fredericks*

Index

Numbers in *italics* indicate illustrations.

Antivenin, 41, 52

Bat, 51
Bear, 49–50
Black mamba, *38*, 39–41
   pictures of, *38*, *40*
Black-necked cobra, 43
Black widow spider,
      28–30

Canine teeth, *14*, 15, 50,
      52
Chelicerae, 30, 52
Cobra, 43–45
Crustaceans, 35, 52

Desert dwellers, 41–42
Digest, 10, 52
Dinosaurs, 20–23
Dogs, 14, 15
Duckbill platypus, 49

Environment, 7, 52
Evolve, 7, 53
Extinct, 7, 53

Fangs. *See also* Canine teeth;
      Molars
   animal categorization,
      12–13
   definition, 53
   desert dwellers, 41–42
   dinosaur, 20–23
   gila monster, 42
   mammals, 47–51
   prehistoric, 17–23
   reasons for, 7–15
   saber-tooth tiger, 19–20
   shrew, 49
   snake, 12, 41, 44, 49
   spiders, 24–31
   underwater creatures,
      33–37

Fangtooth, 35–37
  picture of, *36*
Fernbank Museum of
  Natural History, 21
Funnel web spider, 30–31,
  31

Gila monsters, 41
Giganotosaurus, 21
Grizzly bear, 49–50

Hematoxic, 13, 53
Herbivorous, *22*, 53
Heterodontosaurus, 20–23
Human teeth, *23*

Indian cobra, *43*
Insectivores, 47, 53
Invertebrates, 2, 47, 53

Jurassic Period, 20, 53

La Brea Tar Pits, 18, *19*
Lizard, 20, 41

Mammals, *46*, 47–51
  duckbill platypus, 49
  grizzly bear, 49–50
  shrew, *46*, 47–49
  vampire bat, 51

Metabolism, 48, 53
Molars, 21, *23*, 49, 53

Neurotoxic, 13, 43, 53
Nocturnal, 41, 53

Omnivorous, 49, 54

Pit viper, 8
Platypus, 49
Predatory, 11, 54
Prehistoric, 18, 54

Rabies, 51
Rattlesnake, 8–12, 13
  diamondback, 12
  picture of, *9, 10, 11, 13*
Ringhal cobra, 43

Saber-tooth tiger, *16*, 18–20
  skeleton of, *19*
Shrew, *46*, 48–49
Sloth, 17–18
Skeleton
  giganotosaurus, *21*
  heterodontosaurus, *22*
  saber-tooth tiger, *19*
Snake, 49
  black mamba, *38*, 39–41
  cobra, 43–45

rattlesnake, 8–12, 13

Spiders, 7, 24–31
    black widow, 28–30
    funnel web, 30–31
    tarantula, *6*, 24, 25–28

Spitting cobra, 43–45

Survival, 7, 54

Sydney funnel web spider,
    30–31

Tarantula, *6*, *24*, 25–28
    Mexican red-kneed
      tarantula, *6*, *24*
    pictures of, *6*, *24*, *27*, *28*

Tarantula hawk, 27

Underwater creatures
    fangtooth, 35–37
    viperfish, 33–35

Vampire bat, 51

Venom, 7, 8, 9, 10, 12–13,
    13, 26, 28–29, 30–31,
    41, 42, 43–45, 48–49,
    54

Viperfish, *32*, 33–35
    picture of, *32*, *34*

Wasp, 27

About the Author

Anthony D. Fredericks is a nationally known children's author. His assemblies and school visits have captivated thousands of elementary students and teachers from coast to coast. Fredericks's background includes extensive experience as a classroom teacher, author, professional storyteller, and university specialist in elementary science methods. He has written more than twenty children's books. His Franklin Watts credits include the best-selling *Cannibal Animals: Animals That Eat Their Own Kind* and *Bloodsucking Creatures*. Fredericks is currently a professor of education at York College in York, Pennsylvania.